SONGWRITER'S BOOK

MONICA WELANDER

Hands Up Music

ISBN 978-91-978506-1-2

Published by: Hands Up Music

First edition

2018

Illustrations by © Monica Welander
Proofreading by Garth Simpson

This book comes with a cd: Monica and The Explosion which can be listened to and purchased from www.handsupmusic.se or downloaded from iTunes/Apple music store www.itunes.com

Hands Up Music Kastrullv. 40 S-393 64 Kalmar, Sweden
www.handsupmusic.se

www.monicaandtheexplosion.com/creativesongwriting.html

CONTENTS:

In the beginning there was nothing.
Then I wrote a song.
And now it's here:
Lyrics, melody and rhythm, a story –
all packed together in my own song.
And it can be picked up time after
time; played over and over again.
That's just so cool...

THE SONGWRITER

THIS IS A SONGWRITER

This is a picture of a songwriter who has just completed a new song and therefore is super satisfied and proud.

Just like a sports star that has scored in an important game or won a big championship, the songwriter feels like a winner and does the "V"-sign – V as in Victory.

And the songwriter has reasons to be proud. To write a song is to create something that didn't exist before. It might not become a No. 1 hit, but it was fun to do – so much fun that it makes you want to write more songs.

YOU SET THE RULES

When you write your own songs you are free to create whatever you want, nothing is impossible or wrong.

How can that be? Well, because every single person is unique, and what someone creates from what is inside them is unique and individual for every person.

You are free to create any story, melody, lyrics and rhythm you want to, anything you can come up with. You are also free to make your own rules for how you do it, because when you create something in your own way there is no one else but you who knows what is right or wrong.

You set the rules.

You decide what the songs are going to be like. You have the freedom to write your own songs!

MY STORY

WHY WRITE SONGS?

There are many different reasons why people write songs, and there are different ways to get an idea for a song, and different ways to create it.

Maybe you just think it is fun to write songs, and enjoy it so much that it just happens. Or maybe you have a story to tell – something you have experienced, seen or heard yourself, or just a story that you make up.

Sometimes we write songs because we have something important we want to tell, or have a particular feeling that we want to share but find it hard to talk about, so we express ourselves through music instead.

THE BAND
WE NEED SONGS!

ARE YOU IN A BAND?

Some people start writing songs because they are in a band, or want to start a band, that plays their own songs – originals.

When you are in a band it is possible to write the songs (or parts of the songs) together. Maybe you get an idea for a song while you are jamming together? Some bands write complete songs in the rehearsal studio. In other bands there could be one member who writes the melody and lyrics, and then they work out arrangements of the songs together.

It is up to every band to decide what suits them best, but when you are a songwriter in a group, you have to keep the band in your mind when you are writing.

Ask yourself: What kind of songs suit us? What instruments do we use?

Who are we and what do we want to express through our music?

YES!

OR...YOU JUST WANNA ROCK - OH YEAH!

If you play an instrument or if you are a singer, it is not unusual that you sometimes just want to play around with your instrument or voice because you think it is fun.

Maybe you are trying out new things, and suddenly you discover that you really like what you've come up with. There is something in the music that you find cool, or just gets you hooked and gives you an idea that you can use in a song.

To improvise like this is yet another great way to come up with ideas for new songs.

WHAT IS A SONG?

A SONG IS MUSIC PUT TOGETHER IN A PACKAGE.

Music can be found in so many different forms, long classical pieces that can be played in different ways, improvisatory jazz that is based on jam sessions, or African drumming to mention a few. Even birdsong can be described as music.

But a song has a beginning and an end; it has a frame.

What happens between the opening bars and the final chords is different for all songs. One thing is clear; every song must have a beginning and an end.

Let's start just there. The most important thing when we write songs is to have a frame for the song so we know how it starts and ends.

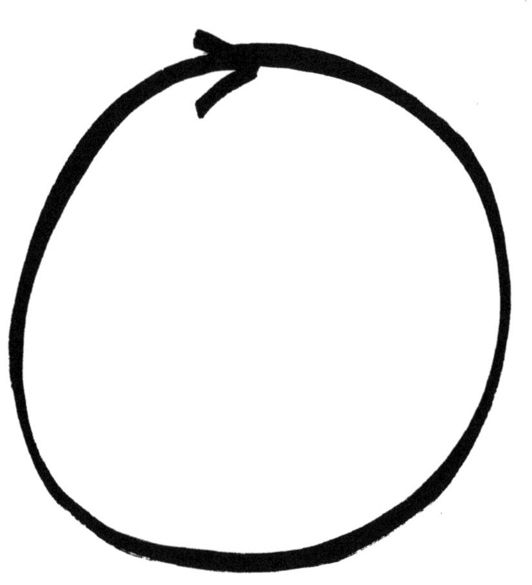

TO TIE UP/LINK THE SONG

A song is also a story. Something is being told through the song, both within the lyrics and the melody. The song starts, something happens and it is all tied up when we come to the end. It is just like when we draw a circle that starts at one point, goes all the way around and joins where it began.

Sometimes we can experience that a song goes around like in a circle very clearly, for example in a melody that wanders off and returns to the same note it started from.

The lyrics can also be built in a way so the song, or every verse, starts and ends with the same lines.

The chorus is a part of the song that is repeated a number of times throughout the song and can also be seen as the core of the song, a summary of what it is about. Many times a song ends with the chorus which is a way to tie up the story and summarise the song.

The song *Save your Whispers* – track 4 on the CD **Monica and The Explosion** (you can listen to all songs from the CD here: www.handsupmusic.se) – starts and ends with the same chord, and in that way follows a circle, it starts and ends at the same point. Starting and ending a song with the same chord or riff is very common in rock and pop songs. It is easy to notice this if you listen to a song over and over again – loop it.

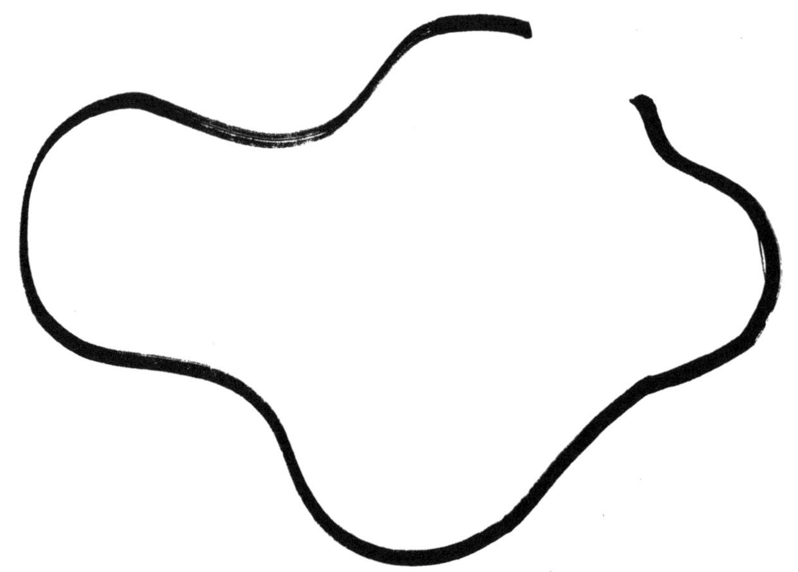

TO MAKE A JUMP

But a song doesn't have to look like a circle; it can look like a roller-coaster, or a toy car race track!

This is a picture of a toy race track. When you build your race track you can build it just how you want it with loops, turns, ups and downs. In the same way you can build your song just how you like it.

Imagine that you take away a piece of the race track and make a jump; you would have to be a pretty good car driver to be able to jump out from the track and then land again on the other side. And you do want to complete the race and reach the finish line as a winner, right?

We can look at the song as if it is a race track, but instead of twists and turns we have verses and choruses.

If we take away a piece of the song and make a jump, that part is then something different than a verse or chorus, we have left the original structure. For example a jump like this in a song can be a solo, a middle eight or a bridge.

A middle eight is neither a verse or a chorus but something that is different, and something new that has not been in the song before. The middle eight is a good opportunity to add something to the song, something to the lyrics that you want to say but could not fit into the verses or the chorus. Just as the name suggests a bridge can connect two different parts of the song. (Learn more about this on page. 39)

When we make a jump in the song it is important to get back to the original structure (for example to a chorus) after the jump, to be able to tie up the song in the end. If we don't return it can be hard for the listener to understand what happened. Just like in a car race we have to make sure that we land on the track again to have a chance to reach the finish line.

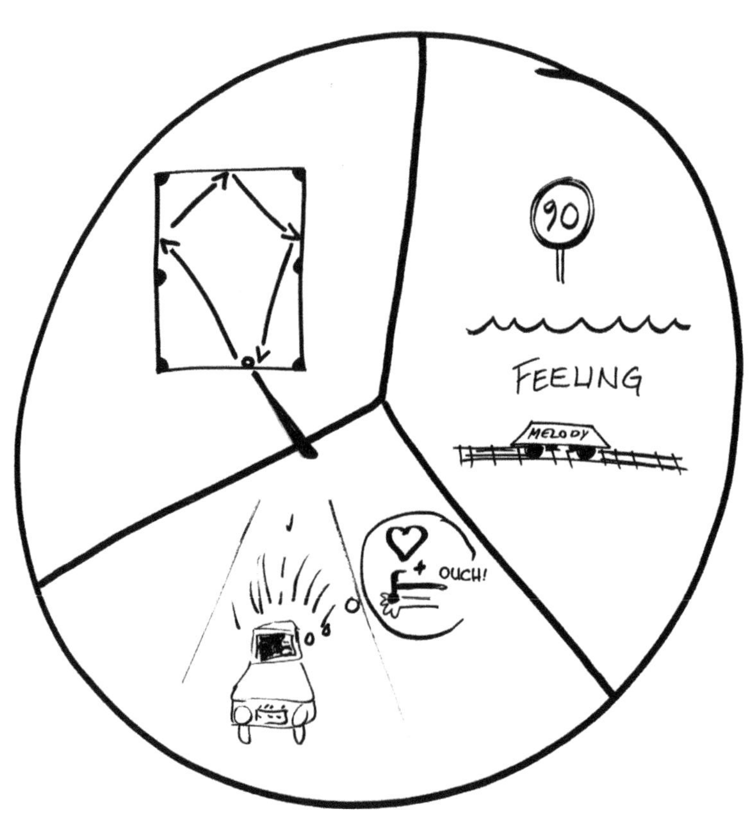
90
FEELING
MELODY
OUCH!

MELODY, LYRICS AND RHYTHM

Songs consists of **melody, lyrics** and **rhythm**.
It can be discussed if it is necessary to have lyrics in a song. There are instrumental songs and some music genres have vocal singing but without words, and can still have a structure, melody and rhythm like songs with lyrics. In this book however, we will focus on songs that have got lyrics, songs within the rock/pop/folk genres.

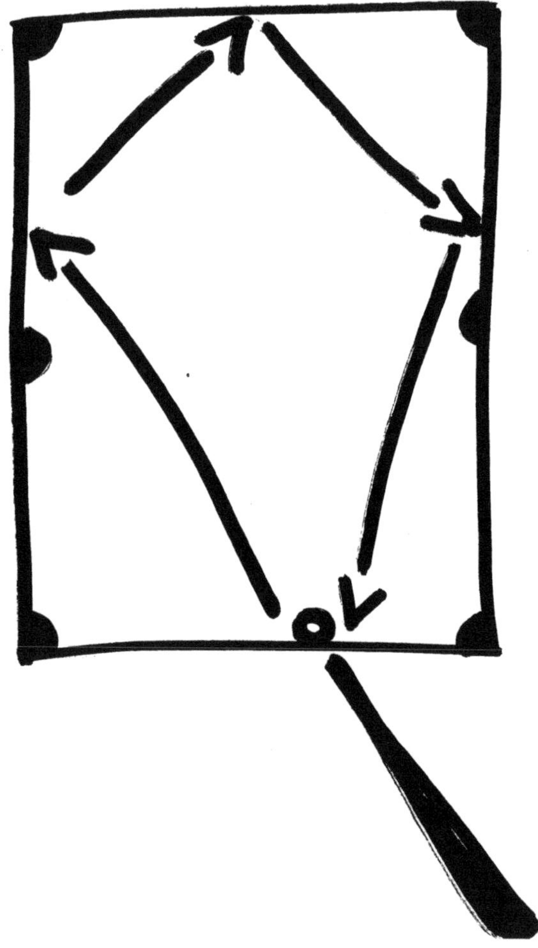

A pool table with four edges that the ball can bounce against.
Or a melody with four notes to choose from.

THE MELODY

The melody in a song is a series, or a chain, of notes that the voice (or an instrument) can follow. Melodies are also found in song intros and solos where an instrument plays a series of notes.

The melody is an important part of the song. Usually if you like the melody – you like the song, even if you don't really understand the lyrics (when the song is in a foreign language for example). But the fact the melody is important doesn't have to mean that it has to be complicated, rather the contrary: the more simple a melody is, the easier it is to remember it, recognise it, sing and play it.

Many of us have probably experienced that we can sing along to a song even the first time we hear it. This must mean that the song has a simple melody, which is great to know when you write songs: it doesn't have to be complicated.

And actually, usually we only need two different melodies to write a basic song; one for the verse and one for the chorus.

Have you ever listened to a recorded song where all the backing instruments are muted so you just hear the vocals? In many rock and pop songs the vocal melody can sound very monotonous without the backing tracks.

I never been to Hollywood
but it sounds so good
Santa Monica Bay big City L.A.
It's like coming back
darling I know this track
I'm not gonna get sacked
Let's get a Cadillac ...

THE LYRICS

The Lyrics put words to the melody so the song gets content, a story and a meaning that we can understand. Though, this doesn't necessarily mean that we understand what the lyrics are about exactly, because the lyrics are only a part of the song and are meant to be performed with music, not as a text that is primarily meant to be read.

But the lyrics are important because they tell the story of the song and what feelings and images the song brings us.

When we humans tell something, we often do so by using just feelings and pictures, for example we describe something that happens and attach a feeling to that. I can describe how I was skateboarding, and because I thought it was fun the words I will use when I talk about it are very positive and maybe I even laugh and smile. It is possible to tell something without any feeling attached, for example reading up the news on TV, but that kind of story telling can be very dry and flat.

To be able to write interesting song lyrics just feelings and pictures are the best material to use. If you do this, you can describe something that is easy for the listener to follow and understand.

And it is easy to think out lyrics if you start describing feelings and pictures when you write.

OUCH!

Imagine a picture, for example of a car, driving fast in the night away from a city. Add a feeling to that picture, "sad" for example. There we have the foundation for a story, the foundation for a song's lyrics. By using our imagination we can create a story and write our lyrics according to what happens in the story. If you get stuck you just have to go back to the picture again and ask yourself: what happened? What did it look like? Who said what? What happened before? And so on.

Many times when I write my songs I start with a feeling, something that makes me want to tell something that I can describe with a picture (or a series of pictures, like a film). Very often the first verse is about a feeling, the second verse about a picture, and the third verse can be something like a summary of how the feeling and picture get linked together and the result of that.

90

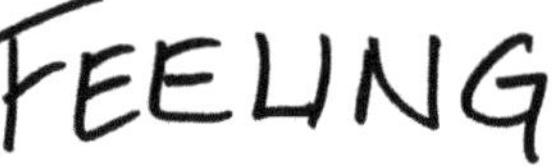
FEELING

MELODY

THE RHYTHM

All songs have rhythm. And the rhythm can be very helpful both for writing the lyrics and building melody.

It is the rhythm that decides how the melody and the lyrics will be presented, the tempo and intensity of the song. You can think of the rhythm like bars or poles that are positioned in a certain order like a pattern, and you place the words and the notes according to these. You can also see the rhythm as a railway track that carries the song, and is essential for the lyrics and the melody to move forward.

The rhythm can also be used to help emphasize the mood of the song. If it is a fast, groovy rhythm it can give you a happy feeling, and if the rhythm is slow and heavy it can express a sad, deep feeling.

If you change the rhythm in a song, it can give you a different feeling and the song can get a completely new meaning and message.

When you get new ideas to melodies, the rhythm often comes at the same time, and it is essential to have a rhythm in the melody to be able to sing or play it. Perhaps we don't think so much about the rhythm when there is a basic one, but many times it is just the rhythm that gives the song its own unique character.

SONG STRUCTURE

Structure means a pattern or a frame for how something is built up.

The structure of a song shows how it is put together by the different parts (verses and choruses for example).

These different parts can be compared to building bricks that we use to build the song with, when writing it.

THE VERSE is often the part that tells the story in the song and brings the story forward.

In the different verses the story can be divided into separate episodes and develop from first to second to third verse for example.

In the song *Hollywood* (track 4 on the CD, lyrics see page 88) you can hear a story that is being told through the verses. (you can listen to all songs from the CD here: www.handsupmusic.se)

THE CHORUS is the part of the song that is repeated several times in the song, and quite often in the same way, or with a slight change.

The chorus usually summarises what the song is about and is the core of the song. In *Hollywood*, which is a song about Hollywood, the word Hollywood is repeated a lot of times in the chorus.

The chorus also serves the purpose to catch the listener's attention. If you write a chorus that is simple, easy to understand and captivating, it becomes easy for the listener to sing along, remember and like the song. If you want to write a real hit you should try not to make the chorus too complicated. Instead, the more simple it is – the better.

These building bricks, the verse and the chorus, are the two most important ones to use in the song. Many times it is enough to build a song with only verses and choruses.

Since it is you, as a songwriter, who decides what the song is going to be like and how you want to create it, it is also you that decides how you want to use the bricks and put them together. You decide what structure your song will have, you set your rules!

Apart from verse and chorus there are other parts in songs that often are used.

AN INTRO is the very first part, an introduction before the song really kicks off. The most common way is to have an instrumental intro (but of course it can have lyrics) that builds up expectations before the first part, a verse for example, starts.

SOLO An Instrumental solo means that an instrument takes a prominent part and plays a melody instead of having someone singing. It is easy to make a solo by keeping the back beat in a verse or chorus but instead of vocals have an instrument playing a melody to the beat. In drum solos there are usually no other instruments.

How long and how many solos there are in songs can vary a lot between different genres. It is not necessary to have a solo, but sometimes it can be good to have a break from the vocals.

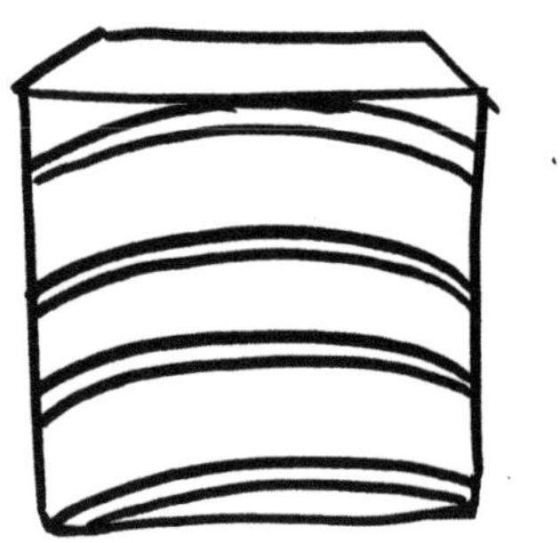

MIDDLE EIGHT A middle eight is a part that stands out from the rest of the song. Something new comes in that has not been there before – it is not a verse or a chorus but has its own lyrics and melody. It is called middle eight because the most common length is eight bars. In the middle eight you have a chance to add something that you think is important to have in the song, but that didn't fit in with the verse or chorus. A middle eight is a good opportunity to do something unexpected and interesting, to raise expectations and make the song more dynamic. I often use the middle eight to add something to the lyrics and the story that I didn't have chance to do earlier in the song. Usually I put the middle eight in the end of the song, for example just before the last chorus.

BRIDGE A bridge is, as the name suggests, something that links two different parts together, for example a middle eight and a chorus. Maybe there is a small gap between the different melodies in these parts, and a bridge can join them together. For example the bridge can have chords that bring the two parts closer to each other. A bridge can also be used in the same way as a middle eight or a riff before a chorus, to raise the expectations before the chorus starts. You can also use a bridge after a solo to find your way back to a verse or a chorus

OUTRO An outro is like an intro but the other way around, an ending of the song. It can be instrumental, or like in *Friday Night* (track 1 on the CD) that has part of the chorus in the outro. (You can listen to all songs from the CD here: www.handsupmusic.se)

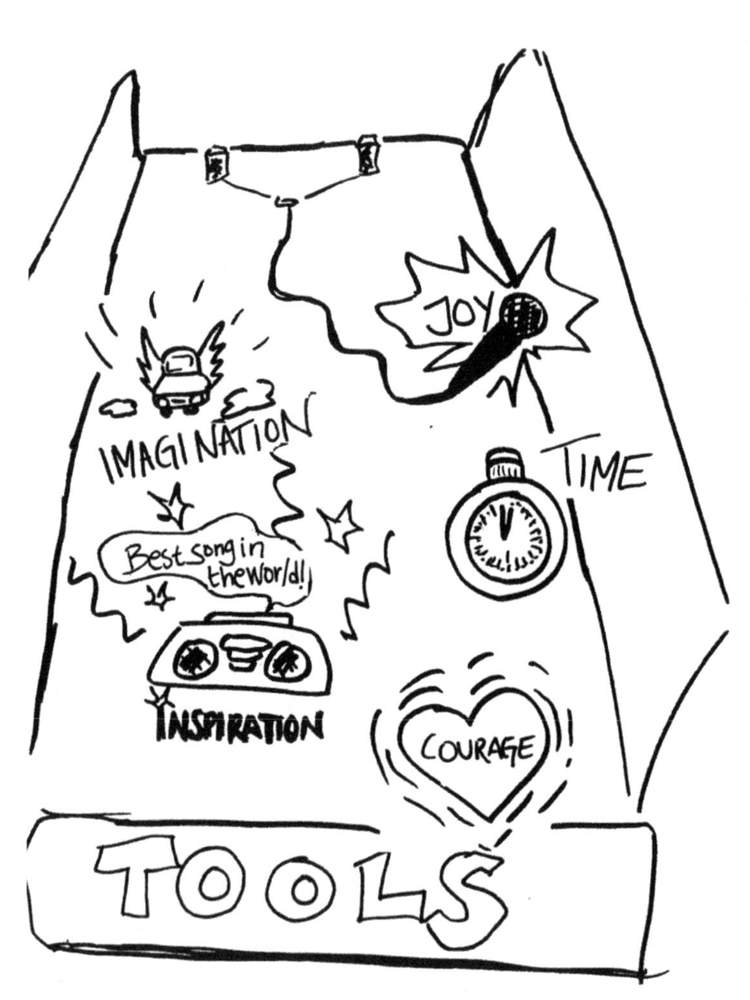
JOY
IMAGINATION
TIME
Best song in the world!
INSPIRATION
COURAGE
TOOLS

THE TOOLBOX

Time, courage, imagination, inspiration and joy are the most important tools for creating a song.

TIME First of all you need time to write, because if you don't have time to write there will not be any songs. When it suits you best to write and for how long you want to do it, is up to you – everyone is different. When I started to write songs I stopped watching TV, and suddenly I had the evenings free for my songwriting. I also thought it was much more fun to do something myself rather than to watch other people doing stuff on TV.

COURAGE You need courage to write good songs.

Courage to write personally, break limits, let loose, do something new, be different, be fun, silly or deep and poetical.

You need courage to create something that is your own and stand up for it, be proud of your work and like it. If you have courage you can be free in your songwriting.

IMAGINATION

JOY

IMAGINATION You also need imagination. Imagination is to be able to create something that does not already exist. It can be to work on ideas and make up something new, and not only limit yourself to what you already know. When it comes to songwriting you need imagination to develop ideas, feelings and experiences and turn them into melodies, stories, lyrics – songs.

JOY There is no point in pushing yourself to write songs if you don't feel like it. There probably will not be any good songs that come out of doing that. But to feel the joy of being creative, that you really feel it is fun and that you enjoy writing, will result in songs that you like, and like to perform, show and share with others.

If it feels boring and heavy when you are working on a song you should perhaps leave that one and start on another one instead. Or let it rest for a couple of days to see if it gets easier, maybe you'll notice that you can change something so that it feels fun and enjoyable again.

INSPIRATION

INSPIRATION can be explained as "something that you experience or feel that makes you want to do something". You can get inspiration to songwriting from your own feelings and experiences, or from something that you see or hear. Maybe you hear a song that you think is really good and you get inspired to make something like that yourself.

Or maybe you meet a fantastic person, hear a funny word, find a cool guitar riff, or that something happens that makes you really angry, and you get inspired to create something out of that.

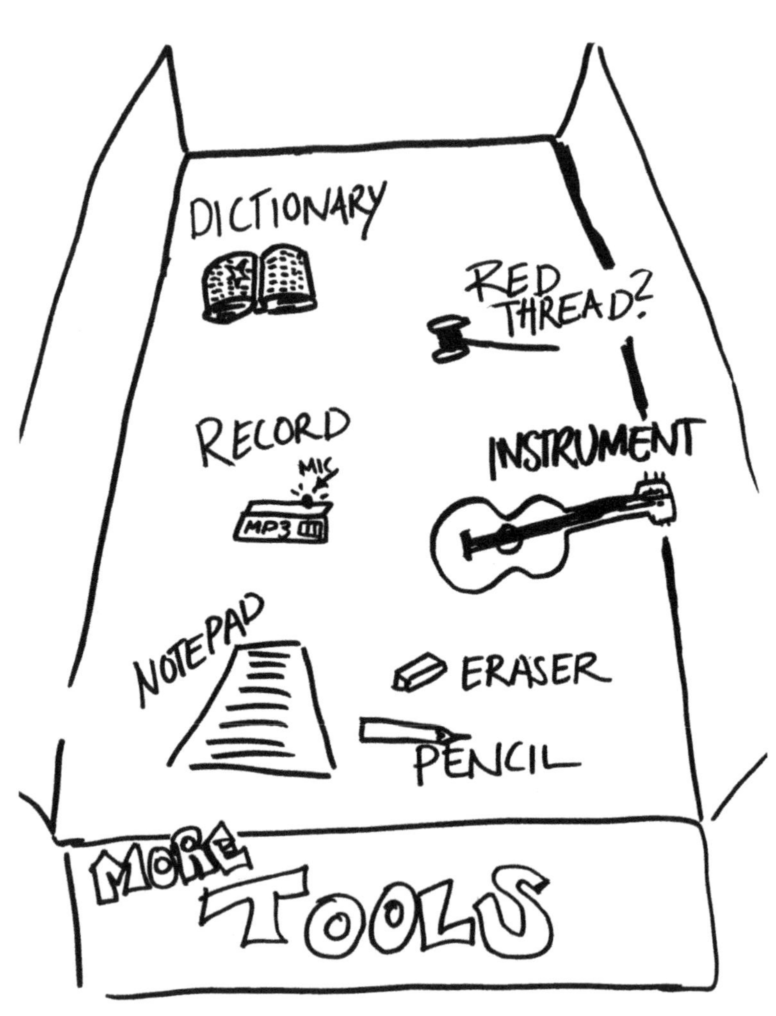
DICTIONARY
RED THREAD?
RECORD
MIC
MP3
INSTRUMENT
NOTEPAD
ERASER
PENCIL
MORE TOOLS

MORE TOOLS!

Piece of paper, pencil, eraser (or mobile phone, tablet). Well it is good to be able to make notes of the ideas you come up with. It is easy to forget, so best thing is to have a piece of paper or a notebook and a pencil ready when you write songs so you can put down lyrics, chords and structure. Many times you get further composing your lyrics when you see the words in front of you; maybe you find that you can rhyme or associate, or you see a pattern in your sentences (to start every sentence with the same word for example).

And the eraser is important too, the more you work on a song and its lyrics, the clearer it gets and sometimes your initial idea of the lyrics needs to change a bit to make the song run smoothly. As a songwriter you are in charge of how you create your songs, and when you are finished with a song. Sometimes it feels right from the start, and sometimes things happen along the process as you write. Just remember that it is your song and it is possible to change it as much as you like until you feel satisfied and that you are done.

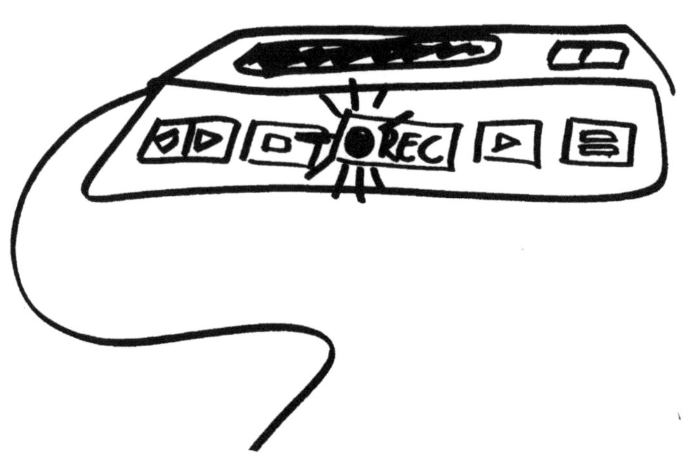
REC

RECORDING

If you know the name of the chords, or if you can write music, it is easy to make notes of the chord pattern and the melody, but nothing is better than to record the song that you have written. You will be able to hear not only the melody, but also how you play the song and use your voice.

It is easy to record songs: you can use an mp3 recorder, a mobile phone, a computer with software for recording, film camera etc. There are many different ways to quickly and easily make a recording these days. What is important is that you record your song in a way that you think is easy and fun, because when it comes to record a song just for remembering it, the quality of the recording is not the important thing, but that it is easily done and doesn't stop your flow.

INSTRUMENT

It is great for your songwriting if you know how to play a self-accompaniment instrument, like guitar or piano. That means you have the possibility to play along yourself as you write and sing the song, working on melody and lyrics at the same time. You don't have to be a very skilled musician to be able to write a good song; even if you only know three or four chords that is actually enough to get you really far. Just check for yourself in song books with well known songs. Many of the greatest hits can be played with only a few easy chords.

If you don't know how to play an instrument maybe you know someone who can accompany you while you are singing the melody, or can show you how to play some basic chords. For some people it is enough to just use their own voice as an instrument, and create the song by singing out melody and lyrics.

DICTIONARY

THERE ARE MORE TOOLS!

A DICTIONARY is useful for writing lyrics. Maybe you need to find a word with a certain meaning that can fit into a rhyme or rhythm, maybe you need synonyms (words with the same meaning) or words that starts with the same syllable etc.

INSPIRING MUSIC Maybe you need to get in the right mood for the song you are working on. Then it could be inspiring to put on some music you like, to kick start your creativity.

A RED THREAD Do you have a red thread in your song? Does it keep together? Do you know what it is about? Can you tie it up in the end feeling that the story has been told? When writing songs, and especially when it comes to the lyrics, it is important that you know for yourself the meaning behind the lyrics. If you know that, things like grammar and how to build correct sentences is not so important, you can actually write your lyrics with only a few key words, fragmentary. If you know the story behind your words it will shine through, so the lyrics get a clear meaning and can be understood anyway.

Pattern for a three chord song

Melody:
Limit yourself to use only three chords: **D, A, G**. Play these chords in a sequence, for example as shown in the song on page 58.

Structure	**Lyrics**
Verse (4 lines)	Feeling
Chorus (3 lines)	Title
Verse (4 lines)	Picture
Chorus (3 lines)	Title
Chorus (3 lines)	Title

EXERCISE: WRITING A SONG

This is a simple exercise to help you get started with songwriting. It is based on a pattern for a song with a basic verse-chorus structure, and a way of composing lyrics and melody as described in this book.

THE STRUCTURE in the song is very basic but it is enough to make it a basic song. The song has two verses and three choruses put together as the pattern shows.

The length of each verse is four lines and the chorus has three lines.

You can also add an intro to the verses. An easy way to do that is to play the first chord during the length of half a verse, for example.

THE MELODY is created by using only three chords. Good chords to start with are D, A, G (see page 91). You decide the order you want to play the chords, and these chords and the way you play them makes a base, a backing beat that helps you find a melody.

THE LYRICS and what the song will be about (the story) is in this exercise created by using a feeling and a picture. The first verse, and the first thing that happens in the song, describes a feeling and the second verse describes a picture.

OUCH!

This is a good way to present the story, to begin with something you can feel and that gives a hint of the mood of the song. Then you tell the story and the reason behind that feeling by describing a picture.

For example we can use the feeling and the picture from the lyrics-chapter. The feeling described there could be hurt or heart broken, and the picture shows a car driving fast out of a city.

We write the first verse about the feeling hurt, and the second verse describes what happens in the picture.

THE CHORUS is often a summary of what the song is about, and is the core of the song. In many songs also the title of the song summarises what it is about (for example: Hollywood and Friday Night) so in this song we can make the chorus so simple that we just use the song title. It can therefore be fairly short.

In the following pages you will see an example of how to write a song by using this pattern (here with a chorus that has a few extra words added), and there is also an example that shows how to add a middle eight and intros to the verses.

HERE COMES THE CHORUS, OH YEAH!

Verse 1

D   A
Here is the first line of the first verse

G   A
Here is the second line of the first verse

D   A
Here is the third line of the first verse

G   A
Here is the fourth line of the first verse

Chorus

G   A
Here comes the chorus

G   A
It   really   rocks us

G   A   D
Here comes the chorus oh yeah

Verse 2

D   A
Here is the first line of the second verse

G   A
Here is the second line of the second verse

D   A
Here is the third line of the second verse

G   A
Here is the fourth line of the second verse

Chorus

G   A
Here comes the chorus

G   A
It   really   rocks us

G   A   D
Here comes the chorus oh yeah

Chorus

G   A
Here comes the chorus

G   A
It   really   rocks us

G   A   D
Here comes the chorus oh yeah

The song above is according to the song pattern described on page 54.

Next page: a version with intros and middle eight.

HERE COMES THE CHORUS, OH YEAH! (VERSION 2)

Intro
```
D                    D
```

Verse 1
```
D                    A
Here is the first line of the first verse
G                       A
Here is the second line of the first verse
D                    A
Here is the third line of the first verse
G                     A
Here is the fourth line of the first verse
```

Chorus
```
G                    A
Here comes the chorus
G               A
It      really     rocks us
G                    A             D
Here comes the chorus oh yeah
```

Intro
```
D                  D
```

Verse 2
```
D                    A
Here is the first line of the second verse
G                       A
Here is the second line of the second verse
D                    A
Here is the third line of the second verse
G                     A
Here is the fourth line of the second verse
```

Middle Eight
```
Em                                A
But there was something more I had to say
Em                           A
Something that can not wait
Em                                   A                    G                      A
Yeah there was something more I had to say so I make middle eight it's not too late!
```

Chorus
```
G               A
Here comes the chorus
G               A
It      really     rocks us
G                    A          D
Here comes the chorus oh yeah
```

Chorus
```
G                    A
Here comes the chorus
G               A
It      really     rocks us
G                    A          D
Here comes the chorus oh yeah
```

REC

WHAT COMES NEXT?

DOCUMENT YOUR SONG

When you are finished with your song it is important that you document it – put the lyrics, the chords and the melody in writing.

It is important that you write in a way so that you can remember it. Even if you can't read sheet music or don't even know the name of the chords you are using, you can still find a way to make notes in your own way, just for you, to remember how to play the song (maybe draw pictures of how you play).

If you can write musical notation it is great for remembering the melody, but to record the song is just as good. If you think that it is a bit hard to write you can always chose to record the song instead and in that way have it documented. But still, it is good to write down the lyrics because there is a risk that you will not hear every word clearly on the recording. And when you actually see the words written down, you might get new ideas and inspiration to help you if you get stuck.

Yes!
Oh yeah...
STUDIO
DO NOT DISTURB!
unless you bring biscuits...
WELCOME

LEARN

Learn, practise, rehearse and perform the song. The next step is to learn the song. Yes, even if you have written it yourself you will have to practise it so that you know how it is meant to be played and sung. Many times it is also while practising the song that you notice new things about it. Things that you might want to emphasise or tone down (find dynamics in the song) to make the story, the feeling and the core of the song even clearer.

If you intend to perform the song in front of people you also have to rehearse it in the way you intend to perform it. This is almost the same thing as learning and practising the song, but when you rehearse for a performance, you need to practise as if you had an audience in front of you. How shall I start the performance? How shall I sit/stand? Where shall I look? If you are going to use a microphone and/or amplifier you also need to rehearse using these, so you feel confident when using them in your performance.

WOW!

THE PERFORMANCE

When it is time for the performance you will surely notice even more things about the song.

Because when you play the song in front of someone you will notice if your intention and message with the song gets through, and if the audience can follow and like it. You will notice this both from how it feels for you, and also the response from the audience.

If you intend to record your song for promotion, publish it, or make a YouTube clip etc. it is always a good idea to perform it in front of an audience first to get some feedback.

Some songs you might need to play many many times in front of an audience before you will find a flow, and feel that you get the meaning of the song through. Don't give up, even if it might feel strange and hard the first time, it will get easier the more you do it!

REGISTERING?
COMPOSER ?
COPYRIGHT?
MONEY ?
ORIGINALWORK?
?
MY OWN SONGS!

PERFORMING RIGHTS ASSOCIATIONS

As a songwriter you can, and you should, join a Performing Rights Association.

In every country there is an association to help songwriters to claim their rights to their own songs. If you join as a member you can register your song title and that you are the composer to the song. By doing this the song and the rights to the song are protected and belong to you so no one else can claim that they have written your song. When you have registered your song you own the rights to it. The association will collect and pay royalties to you whenever your song is being played on the radio, TV, over the internet, or is performed in public. Even live performances, by yourself or somebody else, brings you royalties, so it is a good idea to go out and perform your music live.

Best way to find out more about how to join an association is to look it up on the internet.

Here is a list of some countries' associations:

Australia: APRA/AMCOS

New Zealand: APRA/AMCOS NZ

United Kingdom: PRS For Music

USA: ASCAP,

Canada: SOCAN

MISS
LATE!!!
RUN TOTHEBUS
RAIN...
COINS
WAITINGFORTHE BUS...
BUS STOP
58

EXERCISES: LYRICS

WORD ASSOCIATION Choose a word (or a phrase), and gather a lot of other words and expressions that has a connection to it. Then see if you can make a story of it all.

For Example: Bus stop:

Waiting, bus, bus driver, queue, money, travel card, cold, rainy, being late, street, school, early mornings…

WRITE FOUR LINES where the last words rhyme
(It doesn't have to rhyme perfectly):

First + third line, second + fourth line.

Example:

You are crashing a party
And I am stuck on a bus oh dear
We are going slower than forty
Kilometres per hour I will never get there

FIND ANTONYMS (words that mean the opposite)
The antonyms can be the red thread throughout the song.

Example:

Happy-sad, light-dark, rain-sun, long-short, big-small, soft-hard…

WRITE 3–4 LINES THAT START THE SAME WAY
Example:
I don't wanna go where the rockers go
I don't wanna do what the rockers do
I don't wanna know what the rockers know

I said oh yeah
oh yeah
oh yeah yeah yeah

WRITE THE WORLD'S SHORTEST CHORUS...

WRITE THE WORLD'S SHORTEST VERSE...

WRITE THE WORLD'S MOST DULL, ridiculous, beautiful, honest...verse /chorus

CHOSE A THEME and write a song around that theme. For Example: Love, loneliness, injustice, work, journeys, friendship.

WRITE A SONG WITH THREE VERSES

The first verse describes a feeling, the second a situation, the third verse is the same as the first but with a small change due to what happened in the second verse.

Example:

1. I'm feeling unhappy
I don't want to be
My Honey left me
It feels so empty

2. We sat at the cafe
Where we used to go
He/She said it's over and I think you know
But I just couldn't see

3. I'm feeling unhappy
I don't want to be
My Honey left me
Over a cup of tea

See also *Avenue* (page 86-87 – track 2 on the CD) where the last verse is a slightly changed version of the first. (You can listen to all songs from the CD here: www.handsupmusic.se)

CLAP
MELODY
AFTER
RHYTHM?

EXERCISES: MELODY

MAKE UP NEW MELODIES to familiar songs that you already know.
Listen to a song that you like, sing along but sing with a new melody that fits the song's background beat.

SING A PHRASE (a short sentence) and try different ways.

START WITH A RHYTHM (you can clap, tap or drum the rhythm) and find a melody that fits the rhythm.

START WITH A CHORD and see if you can make a simple melody, or start of a melody with just that one chord. Then add one or two new chords and build the melody that way.

THINK OUT A SONG TITLE and try to find a melody that could suit that title.

LOOP Make a short melody that can be played (looped) time after time.

CONNECT - LINK Make two short melodies that can be linked together: one for the verse and one for the chorus.

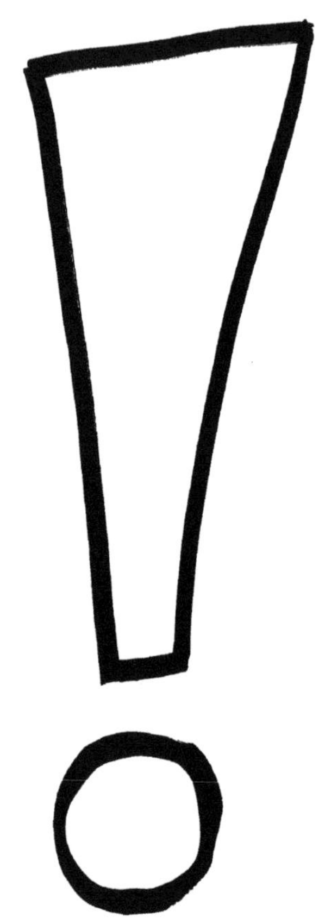

MORE EXERCISES

Here are more exercises to improve your song-writing. It can be both useful and fun to try new ways to write songs and get ideas to songs.

FIRST IMPULSE

COMPOSE FROM YOUR FIRST IMPULSE!

LET THE SONG DEVELOP FROM ITSELF.

For Example:
My first impulse is a lyric line:
"Out on the streets and you can't get away"

I do not yet know what it is that I am about to tell or what that line means, but I can use that line – my first impulse – to make the starting point and foundation I build the song on. (*Who gives a damn* track 5 on the CD. (You can listen to all songs from the CD here: www.handsupmusic.se)

Try to use your first impulse and ask yourself:

What do I mean?
How can I play/sing this?
What story/memory/picture can I find and link to it?
Don't bother about if you from the beginning didn't know where the idea to the song came from, or what the song was going to be about. Just have fun!

La la la...

CHANGE YOUR STYLE!

WRITE A BLUES SONG!

WRITE A MUSICAL SONG!

WRITE A FOLK SONG!

WRITE A PUB ROCK SONG!

WRITE A PUNK SONG!

WRITE A RAP SONG!

PLAY A NEW INSTRUMENT!

SING IN A NEW WAY!

CHANGE YOUR BODY POSITION!

CHANGE TEMPO!

CHANGE LANGUAGE!

TIP:

Listen to others, imitate, do it in a joyful and relaxed way – it is not your usual style so it doesn't really matter what the result is.

JUST HAVE FUN!

MY STORY

THE STORY

TELL A STORY FROM THE BEGINNING TO THE END AND LET THE MUSIC BRING IT OUT.

Begin the story in the first verse and start by writing the first verse.

Continue the story throughout the verses to the end, and finish the story where the song ends.

Let the chorus come in to emphasise the core of the story.

Make some parts of the story extra clear by adding a middle eight.

Start by writing the beginning and finish with the end!

IT'S JUST LIKE THIS

SUPER HONEST

Sometimes it is best to just say exactly how it is.

The notes, the melody and the rhythm will probably come naturally if you write super honest lyrics.

Maybe you write the song…

To someone

With a strong, true feeling

About something that you just have to let out

TIP:

Don't try to make the song a lot more different from how it actually is – it can be long or short, with a lot or with not much lyrics.

Let this be a super honest song with its
OWN structure, length and tempo.

EXAMPLE OF SONG STRUCTURES

FRIDAY NIGHT

(track 1 on the CD. You can listen to all songs here: www.handsupmusic.se)

INTRO
VERSE 1
CHORUS
INTRO
VERSE 2
CHORUS
SOLO 2
MIDDLE EIGHT
INTRO 2
BRIDGE
CHORUS
OUTRO

AVENUE

(track 2 on the CD)

VERSE 1
INTRO
VERSE 2
CHORUS
SOLO
MIDDLE EIGHT
CHORUS
INTRO
VERSE 3

SAVE YOUR WHISPERS

(track 4 on the CD Monica and The Explosion)

INTRO

VERSE 1

CHORUS

VERSE 2

CHORUS

SOLO

CHORUS

BRIDGE/ALTERNATIVE CHORUS

OUTRO

FRIDAY NIGHT

VERSE 1

You're crashing a party and I am stuck on a bus – oh dear!

We're going slower than forty

kilometers per hour – I will never get there!

Just look at my body it won't take you to bed – I swear!

And I will miss you with forty

minutes – you will get hooked and disappear!

CHORUS

Friday Night! I'm begging oh just let me out I got a lot to do

Friday Night! I'm begging oh just let me out I got a lot to do

VERSE 2

I'm out for a party I haven't been for a month – I swear

that I will be the only

one alone and desperate and I fear

I mixed you up with somebody and that won't take you to bed

– or anywhere else no way and I pray

oh God I'm such an idiot just take me away!

CHORUS

Friday Night! I'm begging oh just let me out, I got a lot to do

Friday Night! I'm begging oh just let me out, I got a lot to do

MIDDLE EIGHT

Yeah I said come on and take me away – hey hey hey

I know I prayed take me away but I didn't mean in this way

Cause God I got a brilliant plan but I will be delayed

BRIDGE

God I got a brilliant plan I got a brilliant

God I got a brilliant plan I got a brilliant

God I got a brilliant plan I got a brilliant but I will be delayed!

CHORUS

Friday Night! I'm begging oh just let me out I got a lot to do

Friday Night! I'm begging oh just let me out I got a lot to do

Friday Night! Friday Night!

AVENUE

VERSE 1

I could kill a day for you walking down the same Avenue
To the same bar
I spit on a car
I haven't tasted alcohol, I have to stop and fake a call
You're not that old
I jump on the walls
Hey

VERSE 2

Looking like a summer-night blond in the city lights
You're already inside
Looking out
You cannot be another one, I have to face you on my own
Before the moment is gone
Wish I could tell someone
Wish I could tell someone

CHORUS

My heart is speeding, I don't know if I am breathing
Damn! I'm here again
And I know I know I know I know
I know I know I know – Oh you know
All I wanna say and all I wanna do
Damn! Just take a look at you
And I know I know I know I know
I know I know I know – where to go

MIDDLE EIGHT

Why did you, why did you go out tonight
Why did you, why did you go out tonight
Why did you, why did you go out tonight
Why – alright

CHORUS

My heart is speeding, I don't know if I am breathing
Damn! I'm here again
And I know I know I know I know
I know I know I know – Oh you know
All I wanna say and all I wanna do
Damn! Just take a look at you
And I know I know I know I know
I know I know I know – where to go

VERSE 3

I could kill a day for you walk a mile if I had to
To the same bar
I spit on a car
I have a taste of alcohol, heaven taste like this for sure
This have happened before
I stop at the door

HOLLYWOOD

VERSE 1

I never been to Hollywood but it sounds so good
Santa Monica Bay – Big city L.A
It's like coming back, darling I know this track,
I'm not gonna get sacked,
Let's get a Cadillac

VERSE 2

Up in Beverly Hills now I know how it feels
Famous people in five inch heels, dollar bills
It's like my teenage dream, darling is becoming real
that's me on the screen

CHORUS

In Hollywood, it's the place to be
Hollywood is the place for me
Hollywood is a face you see,
Hollywood is just a face on me –
But oh how it suits, oh how it suits me

VERSE 3

I never been part of the game of beauty and fame

But around here everybody seem to know my name,

I know it sounds insane

It's like coming home, darling I'm known by everyone

I won't be alone

CHORUS

In Hollywood, it's the place to be

Hollywood is the place for me

Hollywood is all fake you see,

But Hollywood could be a break for me –

Hollywood oh it sounds so good

SOLO

BRIDGE/ALTERNATIVE CHORUS

Hollywood, Hollywood, Hollywood oh it sounds so good

Hollywood, Hollywood, Hollywood they never understood

Hollywood, Hollywood, Hollywood,

Hollywood oh it sounds so good

Hollywood, Hollywood oh it sounds so good

SOME BASIC GUITAR CHORDS

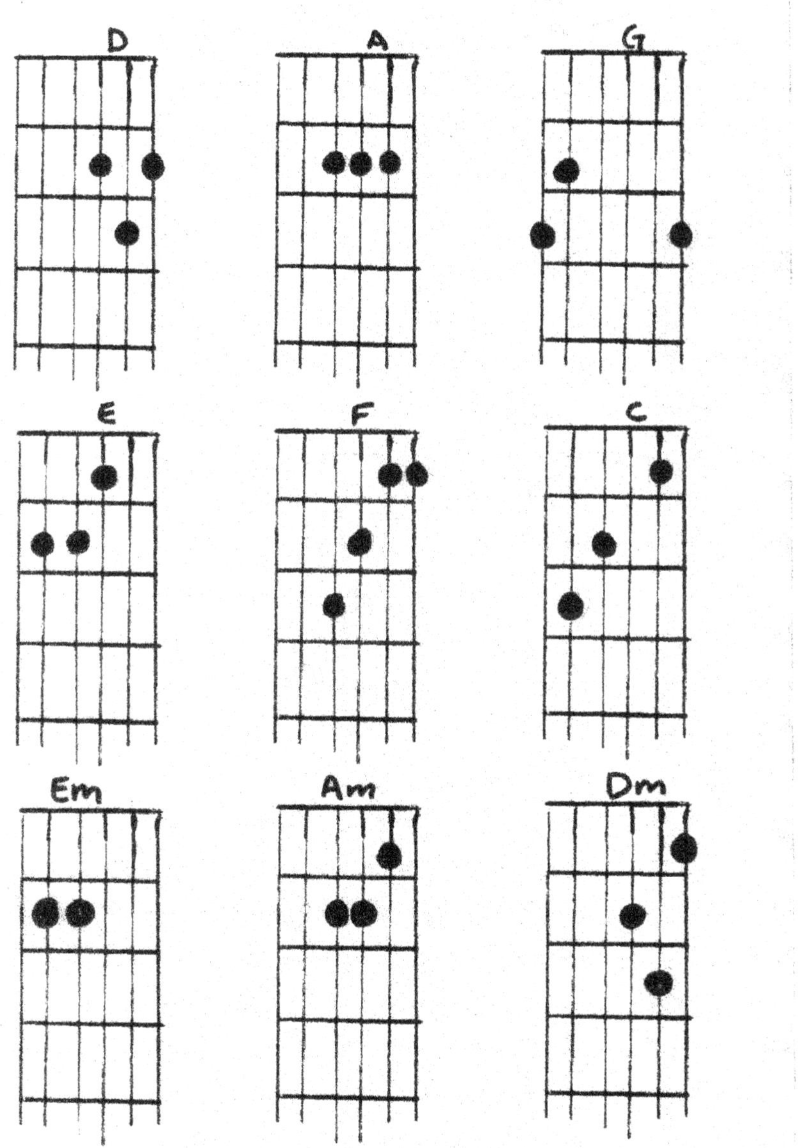

AUTHOR'S NOTE

This book is for inspiration for those who want to write songs. The material in this book is taken from my own songwriting workshops, and is based on my own thoughts and experiences of songwriting.

It is not a book in music theory and it should be used as a practical tool for songwriting along with the CD ***Monica and The Explosion***. (You can **listen** to all songs from the CD here: www.handsupmusic.se)

Every person is unique, and when it comes to being creative, it is important that everyone is free to create in their own unique way – the way that suits them the best.

The CD ***Monica and The Explosion*** can be purchased via webshop:
www.handsupmusic.se
www.monicaandtheexplosion.com
or downloaded from iTunes etc.

Monica Welander was born in 1979 in Sweden.
She is a musician and songwriter performing as **Monica and The Explosion**.

Website **www.monicaandtheexplosion.com**

She started writing songs as a teenager and has been a songwriter and singer in several bands.

She released her debut album *Monica and The Explosion* in 2007. Since then she has been touring intensively around the world as an artist. She has also been active holding songwriting workshops for beginners since 2008.

This book is an updated and improved version in English of her first book *Låtskrivarboken*, published in Swedish in 2009.

For more information about *Songwriter's book* and Monica's workshops:

www.monicaandtheexplosion.com/creativesongwriting.html

www.ingramcontent.com/pod-product-compliance
Ingram Content Group UK Ltd.
Pitfield, Milton Keynes, MK11 3LW, UK
UKHW021653190726
13853UKWH00001B/242